YOU CAN DO BETTER

Healthier, More God-Centered
Relationships in 10 Easy Lessons

KRISTIN N. SPENCER

You Can Do Better: Healthier, More God-Centered
Relationships in 10 Easy Lessons
Copyright © 2019
by Kristin N. Spencer
Imprint of Literary Symmetry

Cover art by Kristin N. Spencer

Scripture taken from the New King James Version®.
Copyright © 1982 by Thomas Nelson. Used by
permission. All rights reserved.

All rights reserved. No part of this book may be
reproduced in any form by any electronic or
mechanical means including photocopying,
recording, or information storage and retrieval
without permission in writing from the author.

ISBN-13: 978-1-951040-03-1
ISBN-10: 1-951040-03-1

On The Web:
http://kristinnspencer.com

Contact the author:
kristin.n.spencer@gmail.com

This book is dedicated to you, the reader.

I applaud your effort to make your relationships better. It is my hope that you when you finish this book, you will understand how embrace and improve your good relationships and step away from the destructive ones.

TABLE OF CONTENTS

INTRODUCTION
1

CHAPTER 1 LESSON ONE: LOVE
5

CHAPTER 2 LESSON TWO: FORGIVENESS
9

CHAPTER 3 LESSON THREE: FULFILLMENT
15

CHAPTER 4 LESSON FOUR: MERCY
21

CHAPTER 5 LESSON FIVE: GRACE
27

CHAPTER 6 LESSON SIX: TRUTH
33

CHAPTER 7 LESSON SEVEN: EXPECTATIONS
39

CHAPTER 8 LESSON EIGHT: HUMILITY
45

CHAPTER 9 LESSON NINE: ACCEPTANCE
                49
CHAPTER 10 LESSON TEN: JESUS
                53
CHAPTER 11 PEARLS BEFORE SWINE: A WARNING
                59
CHAPTER 12 HOLY SEX REBOOT - PREVIEW
                63

INTRODUCTION

<u>Introduction</u>
Think about all of the relationships in your life, good and bad. What if I told you that you could change every single interaction just by reshaping your mindset? Would you be interested? As Christians, we have the most useful piece of living literature available, but when we compile our standards for living healthy and productive lives, we often base our foundations on things outside of the Bible. In just 10 easy lessons, you can change your entire approach to relationships based on an unequivocal truth that will never change and will leave you feeling more fulfilled, accepted, and loved than ever before. From this place of liberty, you can systemically change your interactions and relationships with the people around you.

If you had met me 10 years before, you would not have thought that I would ever be able to write a book about healthy relationships. I was the poster-child for dysfunctional interactions, and almost every single one of my relationships was based on unhealthy principles that I didn't even realize had been part of my learned behavior growing up. After going through a particularly difficult work-place situation with an abusive individual, my mother told me she wanted to talk to me. Our video call went something like this:

"I feel like this is my fault."

"I don't understand, Mom. What are you talking

about?"

"I never taught you how to have boundaries, and because of that, people use you. I think you need to learn how to protect yourself and your family by establishing what kind of behaviors you will and won't accept from people."

"Okay?" I had never heard my mom mention anything about boundaries before in my life.

"Just promise me you'll think about it. If you want a few resources, I have a list."

"Sure, send me what you have."

<u>Boundaries and Personal Worth</u>

As I learned about healthy boundaries, God was also taking me on a journey to find love and acceptance from Him alone (an odyssey I chronicle in *You Aren't Worthless: Unlock the Truth to Godly Confidence*). The culmination of these two learning expeditions led me to place I want to take you as well: establishing and maintaining relationships based on Biblical truth. Though this adventure can seem intimidating, I promise it is well worth the end result.

What about this process seems intimidating? Let me give you an example. If someone wants you to do something sinful, and you choose not to, you will set a boundary and say, "No, I will not do that." They might get angry. You can't control their response, which in this case happens to be anger. But you *can* control whether or not you decide to participate in that sinful activity. This is part of setting a healthy boundary within that relationship. Remember that the point of this guide is to address things from your side, the things you *can* control, not the things you can't control, such as the actions of others. Because of this, each lesson starts with the words, "Today I Choose..." followed by each individual topic.

Going forward, it is important to understand that your worth is not based on your relationships or how other people view you. Your worth is based on God's love for you as His creation. When you keep that in mind, you are able to create boundaries because your worth is not tied up in your relationships or in how others view your worth. If you find yourself having a low-confidence moment, fall back on the following verses and keep pressing forward.

"But as many as received Him, to them He gave the right to become children of God, to those who believe in His name." -John 1:12

"Behold what manner of love the Father has bestowed on us, that we should be called children of God! Therefore the world does not know us, because it did not know Him." -1 John 3:1

I can't wait to take this journey with you as you move forward on this relationship-changing expedition.

Chapter 1

Lesson One: Love

Choose *Love*...

"Love suffers long and is kind; love does not envy; love does not parade itself, is not puffed up; does not behave rudely, does not seek its own, is not provoked, thinks no evil; does not rejoice in iniquity, but rejoices in the truth; bears all things, believes all things, hopes all things, endures all things." -1 Corinthians 13:4-7

Love is precious. There is nothing else like it, and this is especially true when we think about the love of God.

Kristin N. Spencer

Because of how valuable love is, we often think of it as something that we should distribute with caution, measuring out each drop against the amount that has first been given to us. The problem with that way of thinking is that it puts a lot of pressure on our relationships. In fact, that model of love distribution is unbiblical. Love is precious, yes, but we are not limited in how much love God gives us. The love that comes from the Father is unlimited. The verse with which 1 John 4:8 ends is, "God is love." If we realize how infinite God is, we realize that His love is also infinite. God is the source of love.

When we look at love as something to be traded instead of freely given, we become confused about God's plan for love. In 1 Corinthians 13:5, we see that "love does not seek its own." When we only give love in exchange for receiving love, that is exactly what we do, seek our own. Choosing love is a risk. It hurts when we love someone and they don't show us that same love in return. It makes us feel rejected and worthless. But didn't God warn us that would happen? Verses like Luke 10:16 and John 15:18 remind us that when people reject us, they are rejecting Christ, and that if the world hates us we need to remember that they hated Jesus first. Our flesh, the opposite of our spirit, gets angry with us when we love. Have you ever noticed that it feels so much better to hate and become bitter? Think about the last time someone disagreed with you about something you really cared about. Did their actions in that moment make you want to love them more? Probably not. In fact, you might have felt angry and rejected. Those natural feelings, which lead to hatred, are a result of our living in a fallen world. God never encourages hatred. Our Heavenly Father has chosen us as His children. He doesn't want us to wallow in human rejection, when He has paid such a high price to welcome us back into fellowship with Him.

Often, when we hear that something bad has happened to a person that was mean to or betrayed us, we feel happy. We also see in today's verse that, "love does not rejoice in iniquity." Whether our betrayer is dealing with the consequences or their own sin, or that of someone else's, we should never allow ourselves to rejoice or feel happy when sin happens. We must remember that love "bears all things," which means it is our duty as followers of God to listen to and empathize with others when they experience difficulties. And when we listen, we ought to hear, and not to form some sort of argument with whatever that person says.

It is also important to recognize when a relationship has become abusive. In those circumstances we should put distance between ourselves and the abusive person, but that doesn't mean we should stop loving them. We can still pray for them, while we remove ourselves from that abusive person's destructive influence.

Ponder this: How would our actions change if we trusted God to refill any love we passed out, instead of waiting for people to reciprocate (show love back)? What would the church as a body look like if we all chose to love this way? How can this choice affect our witness as we share the gospel with non-believers?

A Missed Opportunity

When I was at Bible college, I noticed that a lot of the women that lived there weren't interested in becoming my friends. I wasn't sure why, but when I moved to Greece and saw missionaries there coming and going, I started to understand a prevailing pattern. Foreign missionaries are people that go to live in a place outside of their homeland, usually for a specified or unspecified amount of time. Because of the constantly changing nature of this vocation/ministry, it is impossible to keep a consistent group of friends. Once you've been a missionary long enough, you know that people leave. It's part of the process. I remember while our family was serving in Greece, my husband had a really good friend whose wife seemed similar to me. We not only shared common interests, but also personality types. For an introvert, there is nothing quite like finding another person that understands that sometimes the hangout has to be over so that a recharge can take place. As this couple's time wound down in Greece, we started to see each other more and more.

One day I told her, "I'm sorry we didn't get to know each other sooner."

The way she responded shocked and saddened me. "Yeah, me too, because we would have been really good friends."

That moment taught me a valuable lesson. It's true that when friends leave, it hurts. But that doesn't mean that we should avoid awesome relationships just because of the pain that separation creates. When we do that, we miss out on a specific type of joy that God provided for us. Love costs us something, yes, but it also gives us something irreplaceable. I will never resist forming another relationship just because I know the other person or I might move away some day.

Prayer Time

Take a few minutes and ask the Lord if there are relationships in your life where you could love in a more generous way. Ask Him to fill you with His love, so that you can give it to others. Pray for Him to help you have wisdom to know how each person in your life needs to be loved by you. Remember that you can always ask God for more love and for comfort when you feel rejected or hated by someone.

CHAPTER 2

LESSON TWO: FORGIVENESS

Choose *Forgiveness*...

"Bearing with one another, and forgiving one another, if anyone has a complaint against another; even as Christ forgave you, so you also must do." -Colossians 3:13
"To the Lord our God belong mercy and forgiveness, though we have rebelled against Him." -Daniel 9:9

Forgiveness is rough. When we receive forgiveness it feels so glorious, but when we need to give forgiveness to someone else, it feels very different. It is important to remember God's forgiveness toward us when we need to forgive others. There have been countless moments in my life when I felt angry that I had to be the one to say "I'm sorry" when the other person sinned against me first. Technically, I wouldn't have responded with a sinful attitude or response if someone hadn't pushed my buttons first. "But God," I would pray, "Do I really need to be the person to apologize first again? That doesn't seem fair. They should apologize to me first since they sinned first." Over and over, I felt the prompting of the Holy Spirit confirm that yes, God wanted me to be the first one to apologize. And then, I needed to be okay even if the other person didn't say they were sorry at all. That doesn't mean we should ignore our hurt feelings. It is healthy and righteous to discuss our feelings. But we need to remember that we can't control the outcome of these discussions, and that means we need to be prepared that the other person may be unrepentant. If that happens, we need to remember that we are still called to forgive. When I am not in a forgiving mood, I pray something like this: "God, please help me to want to forgive them. I know if I'm Your child, that's what I need to do, but I should also *want* to do it because it's the right thing to do according to Your Word."

Ponder this: What expectations do I have for the other person when we sin against each other? What about when someone has sinned against me, but I haven't sinned? How can I model the same forgiveness God has shown me no matter what the circumstances are?

When we are dealing with other believers and they don't follow the model Christ created for us, it feels even worse than if they were an unbeliever. When my kids come to me with a story of how some schoolmate sinned against them, I respond by reminding them that most of the children they go to school with are lost. They don't come from Christian homes, which means they don't know about Jesus. This is a comfort to them, because it reminds them that there is a reason for the child's mean behavior. When we experience conflict or sinful behavior from another believer, there isn't a reason why they shouldn't repent. They know Jesus. They know what He says about sin. It seems like they choose to ignore their need for repentance. For some reason, this feels more personal, as if they want to disobey God because that's just how much they dislike us. But we need to remember that God won't force His children to do things they don't want to do. He doesn't force us to repent when we don't want to, and He offers that same choice to other Christians. It's always sad when Christians hold grudges because it causes division, which God hates. In fact, in Jude 1:18-19, worldly people are described as divisive. That is not how the church of Jesus Christ should behave.

There will be times in all of our lives when we experience someone's bitterness toward us. When that happens, it is important to go to God and ask if there is any unrepentant sin on our part. We can also seek godly counsel on the matter from brothers and sisters we know who love God and study His Word. If it seems that we don't have anything to repent for, we need to remember that it isn't our choice whether others become bitter toward us. In circumstances like that, it is even more important for us to forgive, though we don't have to punish ourselves by giving bitter people more opportunities to slander and curse us. We can speak the truth about the situation, whether or not the bitter person chooses to acknowledge it. After that, it's time to move forward.

Ponder this: When a brother or sister in Christ sins against me, how can I guard my heart against bitterness, knowing how God has instructed them to love? How can I avoid causing division in the body? How can I respond in love when someone has bitterness in their heart toward me? How should I approach non-believers that need forgiveness?

<u>A Regret I'll Never Have</u>

When I first met my father-in-law, he was one of the most cantankerous, argumentative people I had ever encountered. I remember that during those early days, I would go home from visiting my then-boyfriend in tears over some unimportant argument I couldn't seem to avoid having with this man, Allen Spencer. In fact, it seemed like as far as Allen and his family were concerned, everything I did was wrong. Looking back, I can see that I definitely didn't do everything *right*, but there was also no way that every action, word, or intention was *wrong*.

Through the years, I chose forgiveness over and over, never knowing if things would change. I hoped they would, because Allen had had a huge role in shaping the amazing man my husband, Travis, became. Though I didn't understand this at the time, I had taken away my father-in-law's best friend: my husband. As I learned how to be a healthier Christian, unlearning the manipulation I had grown up with, my relationship with Allen improved. In fact, he went from "Allen" to "Dad." We also decided not to talk about politics, and that helped a lot.

Instead of arguing about everything, our relationship shifted, and we were able to teach each other things. But that shift never would have happened if I had held onto every slight, assumption, or lack of grace. The same is true from his perspective, because I had done a lot of things that required forgiveness, too. In 2017, Allen Edward Spencer died suddenly due to complications from a skiing accident. In what we didn't know were the last few years of his life, he was one of my best friends. He would call me once a week to ask me how things were going. We prayed for my husband and my kids together. I miss him every day. It is because we both chose forgiveness that we were able to love each other the way God wanted us to.

Sometimes I think about how our relationship would have stayed the same if we hadn't both forgiven each other, and that thought makes me shudder. I didn't realize it, but we were short on time, and I'm so thankful for the gift that forgiveness gave us. Because we both listened to God's Word, I don't have any regrets about what could have been. What we had was priceless.

Prayer Time

Today focus your prayers on the relationships where you find forgiveness difficult. Ask God to help you see those around you the way He sees them, and to help you forgive each day. Forgiveness is not a one time thing. It takes prayer, effort, and determination to forgive people. In addition to asking for God's grace to cover your forgiveness toward others, pray for God to show you if there is any situation in which you need to ask someone else for forgiveness.

Chapter 3

Lesson Three: Fulfillment

Choose *Fulfillment in Christ*...

"And Jesus said to them, "I am the bread of life. He who comes to Me shall never hunger, and he who believes in Me shall never thirst." -John 6:35
"Jesus answered them, 'Most assuredly, I say to you, whoever commits sin is a slave of sin.'" -John 8:34

Often, our search to find ultimate fulfillment in our

lives through human relationships causes so many problems. Our relational needs can only be met by the love of Jesus Christ. Anytime we look to someone besides Jesus Christ for our fulfillment, it damages that relationship. But why? When we try to find the meaning of life in a relationship with another person, we are asking them to do something that is impossible. We are asking them to love us as if they were Jesus. But no one else is Jesus, and no one on this planet is capable of loving the way that He does. Even your closest friend, your mom, or your brother are incapable of loving you with a perfect love (1 John 4:18).

When we realize relationships are not filling the holes in our hearts, our next idea is to look for fulfillment in things. Food, possessions, goals of success, these are all areas where people seek to qualify their existences as meaningful. And when we seek to place value on our lives through the ownership of objects, the next step is to place more importance on objects than we do on our relationships.

What if you had a friend who was obsessed with magazines? What if every time you got together with them, all they wanted to do was sit and read magazines? They never wanted to talk. They never asked you how you were doing. They never shared anything important about their life with you because all of their time, energy, and extra money was tied up in magazines. You wouldn't call that much of a friendship, would you? In this case, our quest for fulfillment in things will damage our relationships because we are still not fulfilled in Jesus Christ.

We often ignore what God says, "he who believes in me shall never hunger or thirst," and we go out looking for something else. No matter what we find, nothing satisfies us long-term like Jesus does. Nothing gives our lives the same meaning that they have as when we're filled with the love of Jesus Christ. We also find that whatever we have chosen to fulfill us instead of Christ becomes our master. Why is that? In John 8:34 it says that "whoever commits sin is a slave of sin." When we choose something over Christ to give meaning to our lives, we make it into an idol. That is why it feels like we're slaves, because we have chosen sin and made it our master.

Ponder this: What things in my life have I used to give myself purpose? Have I used relationships or things to try to feel fulfilled? What is the only way that my behavior can end if I keep choosing to go in that direction?

Have you ever noticed that the more pressure you put on another person to fulfill you, the more tense the relationship becomes? Even though we may not realize it, when we ask another person to give our life meaning, that unrealistic expectation sucks the life right out of the friendship. Relationships constantly change and adapt because they are based on people. People change over time. It makes sense then, that my relationships may not always change for the better. Then what? The way your relationships grow and change are dependent on how we choose to approach them. Of course, relationships involve two people and two sides, so the other person is able to influence the relationship with their choices as well. But remember that in this book, we are focusing on your side. What can you do to steer your relationship in the righteous direction? If you have a biblical view, you can help steer your friendships in a godly direction before the other person feels too much pressure to make you feel worthy and loved the way only Jesus can.

It feels good when our friends validate our feelings and tell us how much they care for us. But if we depend on those positive affirmations to give our lives meaning, what happens when we have a disagreement? What happens when our friends don't care about us as much as we care about them? God is the only one who will never stop loving us, and He is the only One who will never leave us. In Hebrews 13:5 we are taught that God will never forsake us, but in that same verse it says that we need to be content with what we have. We have God, and He promises to love us and to give our lives meaning. He promises in John 6:35 that if we turn to Him, we will never crave things besides Him.

Ponder this: Am I content with the love God has given me, or do I seek fulfillment and meaning in other relationships? If I choose to accept love and fulfillment from God alone, how would that change my relationships with others?

Letting Go

A few years ago, I started to notice that in a group of our friends, one woman had been recently left out of almost everything. My first reaction was to judge everyone else and condemn them for not being considerate of her feelings. Let's call this friend Annette. I decided to double down on our relationship and invest more of my time and support. If the other people we knew were just going to write her off, fine, but I was going to be an even better friend so that she wouldn't feel it as keenly. Fast forward several months and I could predict exactly how every single one of our conversations would go. Then I would get into a fight with my husband about it.

"Did she even ask you how you're doing?" Travis rolled his eyes.

"Of course." I twisted the dead skin next to one of my fingernails.

"But you didn't talk much about what's going on with you, right? Babe, you look awful."

"Gee, thanks." I wanted to wince, but I knew he was right. I felt as awful as I'm sure I looked.

"Every time you talk to her, you get completely drained. What was the crisis this time?"

"Same thing as always."

"You have to stop doing this, Kristin. It isn't good for you. You've shared with her what the Bible says over and over again, and she doesn't want to hear it. You need to have people in your life that pour back into you. It's not fair for you to be the one doing all the pouring out. This isn't your burden to bear. She needs to hand it over to Jesus."

It only took about five more similar conversations with Annette for me to accept that Travis was right. I wasn't helping her, and she sure wasn't helping me. No matter how much I wanted to be there for her, I couldn't give her life meaning. I couldn't fulfill her. Only Jesus could do that. And because she placed that pressure on me, our relationship fell apart. I still pray for her and I still love her, but until she realizes that only Jesus can fulfill her, we can't be friends.

Prayer Time

Today, before you pray, take the time to re-read the verses for this section, and look up the verses I mentioned in the text. Ask God to make those verses real in your life. Ask God to show you if any of the relationships in your life have become idols that are damaging your relationship with Him. As always, I'm praying for you!

Chapter 4

LESSON FOUR: MERCY

Choose *Mercy*...

"But God, who is rich in mercy, because of His great love with which He loved us, even when we were dead in trespasses, made us alive together with Christ by grace you have been saved." -Ephesians 2:4-5

"Righteousness and justice are the foundation of Your throne; Mercy and truth go before Your face." -Psalm 89:14

Mercy is the magic pixie dust that makes all of our relationships sparkle. Any relationship you sprinkle mercy on will become more compassion and empathy-centered. We all need mercy from God. But what does mercy mean? One way it is defined is as kindness and compassion toward those who are needy. When sick people went to Jesus for healing, they often asked Him to have mercy on them (Matthew 9:27, Luke 18:38-39). Mercy also comes as an opportunity to avoid the punishment we deserve. As we see in Ephesians 2:4-5, though we deserved death because of our sin, God who is rich in mercy and love, kept us alive in Christ Jesus. We can choose to reject Jesus' sacrifice, but if we do that, we are also rejecting God's mercy.

What role does mercy play in our earthly relationships? When you know a friend has been going through a rough time and they seem distant or angry, you have the opportunity to show them mercy. During this season they may say an unkind thing or ignore you for a while. But you can choose to respond with kindness, because you know they are needy. Mercy in this situation might look like this, "Hey Jane, I know that you have been having a hard time lately. I just want you to know I'm here for you—whenever—if you want to talk. I care about you."

It could also be that your friend or family member has made a huge mistake. They have done something that hurt you, and others have encouraged you to make them pay. But because you know Jesus has died for their sins, including the sins they have sinned against you, it is better to show them mercy and let God sort out the consequences that they will face. Whether the offender apologizes or not, you can still choose to respond in kindness.

Ponder this: Has there been a chance to display mercy in any of your relationships lately? Do you remember a time in one of your relationships where another person showed you mercy? How did that feel?

One of the natural benefits of choosing to display mercy in your relationships is that whatever trust is there will increase. In Psalm 89:14 we see that truth and mercy are besties. The reason why mercy and truth get along so well together is that mercy, kindness in a time of need, is an action that displays the truth, "When you are having difficulties, I will still be here, and I will be kind, even if you aren't." People often say that when you go through hardships, you learn who your real friends are. Mercy is the reason for this. When we experience trials or grief, our flesh screams out for sinful relief, and we are not usually the best version of ourselves. It takes additional prayer, time in God's Word, and buckets full of self-control to make righteous choices when we are under a lot of stress. Mercy leaves room in our relationships for understanding and imperfection during the difficult trials God uses to shape who we are in Christ. I'm certainly not perfect, and I cherish those moments of mercy when the people I love show me love whenever I'm grumpy, angry, or sad. It is important to remember that mercy is not an excuse to sin, but it is an option for how to deal with sin when we know a person we love is struggling. Thank the Lord that His mercies for us are new each day (Lamentations 3:22-23).

Ponder this: How has God shown us mercy? Does His mercy for us ever run out? How can we apply God's endless mercy to our relationships with others?

<u>You Did It All Wrong</u>
One of the things God has called me to do with my life is to walk alongside survivors of abuse as a friend and support person. Many times, this puts me in the unique position of being one of the first people that they feel comfortable being completely honest with. I

remember that one time, I got an email from a friend who had just learned how to say "no." In this email, she had chronicled every word, action, and train of thought I had had in our previous conversation, and made notes about why everything I did was wrong. My first reaction was offense. How dare she! I was spending time with her, trying to support her and help her sort through her feelings, and she wrote me this email with a list of all my shortcomings and mistakes. In fact, she had even made some rather grand, incorrect suppositions about what I had meant when I said certain things.

Before I started writing down the long list I had been mentally accumulating in my head while reading this email, I felt God prompting me to pray. I knew that my friend was going through a lot, and she needed mercy. But certainly there was still room in the realm of mercy to remind her that I was her friend, and maybe she shouldn't write me such rude emails. God is so good. He reminded me that this wonderful friend had just learned how to say "no," and also how to voice her opinions. The fact that she felt comfortable enough with me to critique our conversation was a reason to rejoice, not to get upset. She was making progress. I just needed to get over myself and accept that maybe some of the things in the email were true, and others that weren't—there was no need to defend myself.

When she said sorry for the harsh tone of her email the next time I saw her, I told her there was no need to apologize. God was helping her express herself in an honest way without being overly concerned about the other person's response. I shared my initial reaction with her, God's response, and told her she could practice on me anytime. We both had a good laugh, and our friendship grew more intimate as a result. She knew she could trust me to share her real feelings with me because God had told me to show her mercy.

Prayer Time

Take some time in prayer today to thank God for His mercy. Ask Him to help you be more merciful, and to have wisdom to see the circumstances in your relationships that require more mercy. Think about the people in your life that display mercy on a regular basis and pray for them to continue to be strong in the Lord. Being merciful is hard work, and requires the specific help that comes through prayer.

Chapter 5

LESSON FIVE: GRACE

Choose *Grace*...

"And He said to me, 'My grace is sufficient for you, for My strength is made perfect in weakness.' Therefore most gladly I will rather boast in my infirmities, that the power of Christ may rest upon me." -2 Corinthians 12:9

"As each one has received a gift, minister it to one another, as good stewards of the manifold grace of God." -1 Peter 4:10

When we looked at mercy, we discussed how mercy creates opportunities for imperfection during a time of need. One of the natural results of giving another person mercy is increased trust. Grace also increases trust because it creates an opportunity for imperfection, without automatic rejection, in our relationships. Look at 2 Corinthians 12:9. God's grace, often defined as undeserved favor toward men, is sufficient. That means it keeps us going. Have you ever had a really bad day? Has something discouraging happened that made you feel like you couldn't keep going? That is what Paul was describing in this verse. He had been going through a health crisis and kept asking God to heal him, but God said "no." In this verse, Paul tell us that God said, "My grace is sufficient for you." So when we go through trials, God's favor and His love will sustain us. They will keep us going. Grace is what reminds us that we can't do anything to earn love from God. He already loves us, and when we make mistakes, He still loves us. That's what grace means.

Ponder this: How can we apply the principle of God's grace to our relationships? Is there some unspoken requirement we have for our relationships? Do we have mental mandates that must be met in order for us to love the other person? Or do we choose to extend grace to our friends and family?

What does grace look like in our everyday life? Our salvation is a result of God's grace, His favor toward us. Our spiritual gifts are a result of God's grace. We don't deserve them. But how does grace shape our relationships with other people? I think an important question to ask in each of our relationships is, "Why do I love this person?" Is it because I'm extending God's grace to them (meaning that there isn't any one particular thing they can do to earn my love)? Or is there a secret checklist I go through in my head based on what they offer me when I'm deciding whether or not I love them? In 1 Peter 4:10, it says that we should give each other the same gifts God has given us. That includes grace. I work with a lot of people that have experienced some kind of intense difficulty in their lives, and grace is what makes my relationship with them a safe place. They know I love them based on God's love, which means I also approach them with personal grace based on God's grace. There isn't anything they can do to earn my love. I already love them because God loves them. There isn't anything they can do to lose my love, because it isn't based on what they do or don't do for me. But I didn't always approach my relationships that way. Refusing to extend God's grace to my friends the same way God extends His grace to me damaged many of my relationships; some beyond the point of repair. Do you have any friends that treat you differently depending on what you give them or do for them? That isn't grace, that's selfishness. But even when we experience selfishness, we can still choose grace from our side.

Ponder this: How can I use grace to make my relationships with other people a safe place for them? How does giving others grace reflect my relationship with God? What would it look like if I used mercy and grace in my relationships to increase trust between me and the other person? Why should I share the grace, love, and gifts God has given me with others?

I Feel Bad For Them

When I think about the concept of grace, I can't help but think of my children: three little (well, not so little anymore) blessings God uses daily to remind me of how much I need Him and how much He loves me. Travis and I have worked very hard not to have one of those lists for our children. You know the kind I mean, right? A list of all the things that our children have to do before we give them unhindered love and approval. But as they get older, my kids are starting to notice the expectations that their friends' parents have for their children. Last week, I had a very depressing conversation with my 10-year-old.

"Mom, I got a B on my math test."

"Great! Good job, honey."

"Aren't you mad that I didn't get an A?" Her big hazel eyes grew wide.

"Well, did you do your best? Did you study?"

"Yes."

"Then why would I be mad?"

She sighed in relief. "It's just that..."

"Yeah?"

"I have some friends... their parents get mad if they don't get all A's."

"Daddy and I don't care about the grades you guys get. You know that. If you get a low grade, we might need to get you some help so that you understand, but that's the only reason we need to know."

"But some of my friends have to get all A's."

"Well, that's between them and their parents, but Daddy and I will never treat you that way. We want you to do your best, but that isn't the same as wanting you to get a certain grade."

"You know what, Mom?"

"What, honey?"

"I feel bad for them."

"Me, too."

The simple truth is that a lot of people in this world are only interested in the end results, which means their love is also based on the works (AKA actions and abilities) of others. When we show our kids, our friends, our spouses, our whatever-elses that we choose grace, we stick out. Grace isn't the norm. I hope that someday we can change that.

Prayer Time

Grace is such an important part of our relationship with God. Take some time to think about God's grace for you and thank Him for it. Grace can transform our relationships with our family and friends. Pray that God will help you to understand how you can show grace to others, and to love them without requiring anything from them in return.

CHAPTER 6

LESSON SIX: TRUTH

Choose Truth...

"My little children, let us not love in word or in tongue, but in deed and in truth." -1 John 3:18
"And you shall know the truth, and the truth shall make you free." -John 8:32

Have you ever heard the saying that truth is relative? That's a lie according to God's Word. Truth is good, truth is loving, and truth honors God. Think about how normal it has become to lie. When someone asks you, "How are you doing?" you usually answer, "Fine." We use that question and answer as a greeting in everyday communication, but if we aren't fine, then that's a lie. Deception and concealment are built into all of our relationships, and we have to work extremely hard to kill lies in our thoughts and speech before we can begin to eliminate them from our friendships.

When we talked about mercy and grace, we said that these two things are trust builders. But there are other things we can do in our relationships to build trust and reemphasize truth. In 1 John 3:18, we see that we are to love others "in deed and in truth." From our side, it is important that we cultivate truthful behavior by taking every thought captive (2 Corinthians 10:4-5). I have struggled with this specific issue, and it's something I still struggle to keep under control. I used to think it was okay to exaggerate stories so that people would pay attention to what I was saying. That's lying. When we add to the truth, it becomes a lie. When we want to gain attention so badly that we are willing to change even small details of what really happened, that is a problem. It means we are looking outside of our relationship with Christ for fulfillment. There are many reasons why people lie, but the main one is related to pride. Did I leave a truth out when I explained something to my friend because I was afraid they would think less of me? That's pride. Did I over-embellish my abilities to gain someone's respect? That's pride. Pride is a relationship killer. But truth has the potential to deepen and enhance your friendships and family relationships.

Ponder this: Why is the truth so important in our relationships? How does truth affect my relationship with God?

One of the most important aspects of truth is its ability to liberate; to set free. Look above at verse John 8:32. What does that mean on a practical, relational level? Have you ever felt trapped or constrained because you didn't have a person to trust with your most vulnerable feelings? I definitely have. When we finally find a friend or have a safe family relationship where we can share our innermost desires and darkest truths without fear of loss of that person's love, it frees us. We feel joy and release. And even when these special friends give us a loving rebuke or criticism, we trust that they are doing it because they care for us. Truth spoken in love doesn't have the same sting as it does when we've heard truth in a judgmental and hateful way. Have you ever heard the saying, "They stabbed me in the face," and wondered what it meant? It means that someone has told you a truth that is difficult to hear, but they gave you the courtesy of saying it to you in love, instead of gossiping about your faults behind your back (hence, "stabbed me in the back"). In Proverbs 27:6 we see that though a rebuke may sting when coming from a friend, it is beneficial, "Faithful are the wounds of a friend, But the kisses of an enemy are deceitful."

When we are passionate about truth, the things we say mean more. When someone else knows that I value truth, they will believe me when I say that they can trust me. Remember what 1 John 3:18 says, that truth exists when we love in word, tongue, and deed. Do my actions match up to my words? Are my words loving? Do I carefully choose the words that roll off of my tongue so that people will know I love them? Sometimes it is tempting to beat people over the head with the truth. Just because what we say is true, it doesn't mean we've said it in a loving way. What if you had a friend who was wearing something revealing, and you knew she was usually very modest? Would you yell out how inappropriate her clothing is, or would you take her aside to let her know she might want to reconsider what she's wearing? What if she didn't realize her shirt was see-through and you yelled that out in front of everyone? She would be so embarrassed, and not because of her clothing choices, but because of the way you pointed it out to everyone in an inconsiderate way. We need to remember to share the truth in love at all times. This kind of caution creates a trusting environment where your relationships have the opportunity to thrive and grow.

Ponder this: How does the truth liberate us? How can the freedom that comes from truth be beneficial to our relationships? How can I create a loving, trusting place for my relationships to flourish? Have there been times in my past when I could have been more careful with my words? How can I avoid speaking the truth without love?

<u>Truth I Should I Have Kept to Myself</u>

I went to a magnet high school in Southern California where there weren't really any social groups. The benefit of that type of environment was that you could accumulate a ton of friends, because you automatically had intellectual interests in common with every person there. Enter Mateo, a sweet guy who liked a lot of the same music I was obsessed with at the time. We would talk on the phone and at school. Then he shared a secret with me, he had a crush on our mutual friend. Prom was coming up, and he wanted to ask her, but he was afraid. I knew that the odds of her saying yes to his invitation were high because she had told me she didn't really want to go with anyone that had already asked her. If only she could somehow find out that he wanted to take her as his date. I'm sure you see where I'm going.

"But she's going to prom with you. I don't

understand why you're so mad."

"Kristin, I told you I liked her in confidence. You totally betrayed my trust. Now she knows I like her and she doesn't like me back. Prom is going to be totally awkward!"

"You're right, Mateo, I'm sorry. I promise I won't ever do anything like this again. Can't you forgive me?"

"No."

And he didn't. He ignored me for the last two months of our senior year, and someone who had been my friend since early freshman year wouldn't even look at me, much less talk to me. My betrayal of his trust ended our friendship forever.

Not only was our friendship over, but I had become a really strong Christian my senior year of high school, and the way I had behaved reflected negatively on Mateo's view of Jesus Christ. I had been trying to help Mateo, but in my own selfish way. It was his secret to share or to keep, and I had taken that choice away from him. The trust of another person is precious, and should be treated as such. It was a lesson I should have learned back then, but it took several other big relationship blunders before I finally understood how important trust is.

Prayer Time

Ask God to help you put these verses into action in your life. Start to take time in prayer each day to ask God to help you care about truth as much as He does. Confess to God if you have a problem lying, and ask for His forgiveness. Pray whether there are any confessions you need to make to other people in your life that you have deceived or lied to, or if you have used words to shame instead of shedding truth in love and need to apologize.

A Note about Manipulative Relationships

Kristin N. Spencer

I pray you haven't experienced this, but sometimes Christians will use these verses to demand that you tell them every detail in your life so that they can use those facts against you to manipulate you. That is not a biblical position. Remember that every believer should approach your truths with love, and not use the details you have trusted them with against you to get you to do something for them. Sometimes friends also get angry if you share your truths with another friend because they want exclusivity (they don't want you to have a close friendship with anyone besides them). This is also manipulative because what they are really trying to do is find fulfillment in your friendship, instead of in Jesus Christ, by making sure your friendship with them is your most important friendship. It is also wrong for you to do this to another person. Remember, truth must be loving, not selfish.

Chapter 7

Lesson Seven: Expectations

Choose *Realistic Expectations*...

"The hope of the righteous will be gladness, But the expectation of the wicked will perish." -Proverbs 10:28
"My soul, wait silently for God alone, For my expectation is from Him." -Psalm 62:5

Unrealistic expectations have ruined many friendships and other important relationships. When we talked about fulfillment, we said that according to the Bible, it is wrong to attempt to find fulfillment by any means other than the love of Jesus Christ. The expectation that another person will give your life meaning the way Jesus can is one of the biggest reasons for relationship breakdown. Remember, no one else can fulfill us besides Jesus. However, there are other unrealistic expectations that may cause us grief. According to Proverbs 10:28, "the expectation of the wicked will perish." We know that our hearts are naturally wicked (Jeremiah 17:9), which means that our expectations, apart from God, are "of the wicked." The only way to change that is to measure our expectations against God's Word. So let's examine a few unrealistic expectations (besides fulfillment, which we already talked about) that plague many of our relationships.

The first one to examine is, "I expect my friends/family to help me as much as I help them." Though the Bible does teach us that we should treat others as we want to be treated (Luke 6:31), it does not instruct us to keep a record so that everything is fair and even. We are instructed in Psalm 62:5 that our only expectation should be from God. We expect God to help us. That doesn't always translate into "God helps me the exact way I want help," but we can expect help from Him in general. Expecting others to match everything we have done for them can be a huge drain on any relationship. When we do that, we are only doing good deeds because we want something in return. Love doesn't work that way because as we see in 1 Corinthians 13:5, "love does not seek its own."

A second unrealistic expectation is that another person will hold your opinions as high as their own. Have you ever had someone give you advice when you didn't ask for it? How did that make you feel? In my life, the friendships that I have treasured the most are the ones where my friend has waited until I asked for advice, and then pointed me to the Bible so that I could form a godly opinion. When we expect our friends and family to adopt our opinions just because they are our opinions, we create a hostile environment where they aren't free to form their own opinions. That kind of relationship is stifling to both people involved.

The next unrealistic expectation we will discuss (there are too many to mention them all in a small devotional like this one) has to do with unwavering loyalty. For some reason, we expect our friends and family to be completely loyal to us even when we are wrong. We should hope that all of the Christians we know are loyal to God above anyone else. We should also understand that people who don't follow God may not feel any amount of loyalty to anyone besides themselves. When one person says something rude to us, we expect all of friends to be rude to them in return. The problem is, that isn't the biblical thing to do. If we are truly loyal to God, we should love our enemies, and the enemies of our friends. That doesn't mean we accept their sinful behavior, but that we choose to love them in spite of it. I think we need to make more of an effort in our relationships to stay loyal to God, and not pressure our friends and family to maintain this unbiblical attempt at dispensing justice. It is especially important to understand that when we are in sin, we need our friends to break their loyalty to us, so they can confront us with this sin, and we might reconcile with God.

Ponder this: Are there any unrealistic expectations that I assume my friends should follow? What does God's Word say about where my expectations should be? Why is it unloving to have unrealistic expectations from others according to 1 Corinthians 13:5?

Another unrealistic expectation we often have in our relationships is that we expect others to be able to understand our expectations without telling them what those expectations are. When we do that, we assume our friends and family can read our minds. That is insane. That is why it is important to communicate what our expectations are, so that there are fewer misunderstandings or hurt feelings. We also assume we can read the minds of others, and most of the time, we put the most horrible version of what they could be thinking into our minds as the most logical explanation. "Well she didn't call me back, so that means she doesn't want to be my friend anymore." That's an assumption. A lot of the problems in our relationships could be easily solved through clear communication. It is unrealistic to expect that we know what another is thinking or feeling, or that they know what we think or feel if we have not communicated.

Ponder this: What reasonable expectations do I have for my relationships? How can I communicate them with my friends and family in a loving way?

Like You Never Stopped

One of the most precious types of friendship I have experienced is long-distance and judgment-free. When you live and serve in different countries, you will inevitably make friends with people that you can't stay close to geographically. But even if you live in the same country, God will usually pull people in different directions as various needs arise. Last month, we had friends visit from Serbia, and it was one of the best times of fellowship we've had in a long time. We were all talking one morning and my friend asked me about the last time I talked to a mutual friend in a third, and different country.

"Oh, I haven't talked to her since before she went to visit you guys. I bet you know more about what's going on right now than I do. But we'll talk again soon."

"I just love those types of friendships. Isn't it so cool

how you can not talk to them forever, and then when you talk again it's like you never stopped?"

"It's the best. But I don't have a lot of friendships like that." I sighed a happy sigh as I thought of my far-away friend.

"Me either, it seems like some people get so upset when you don't check in with them every couple of weeks." My friend sighed a not-so-happy sigh.

"Well, it takes really confident people to maintain long-distance relationships where you don't talk often."

"What do you mean?" She looked at me, patiently waiting for my answer.

"Some people take it personally and think that you stopped wanting to be friends with them, when really, it's just that you're both busy. You still love each other. But in order for that kind of relationship to work, both people have to be confident that a pause in communication doesn't have any underlying implications."

"Huh. That makes sense."

"And that's why you can pick up like you never stopped talking."

"I wish more people approached relationships that way."

"Yeah, me too." I thought of all the people that had dropped me when I had moved overseas, but instead of being sad, I was grateful for the friends, like our friends from Serbia, that we have confident and understanding relationships with.

Prayer Time

In a world that is so self-focused, it is easy to demand things from the people around you. Ask God to help you recognize which expectations are realistic, and which ones are unrealistic. Make a list if necessary. Pray that God will show you how to communicate, and to understand that it is equally important to ask those we have relationships with what they expect from us. Even if they don't have realistic expectations, then you will have an opportunity to talk about why their expectations are unrealistic. Pray for wisdom to know how God's Word applies to each expectation.

CHAPTER 8

LESSON EIGHT: HUMILITY

Choose *Humility*...

"But He gives more grace. Therefore He says: 'God resists the proud, But gives grace to the humble.' Therefore submit to God. Resist the devil and he will flee from you." -James 4:6-7

I've written a whole book about humility, pride, and worth. I could probably write ten or twenty more and still not have written everything there is to be said about the importance of humility. Humility is underrated. It's the underdog. Humility is one of the least popular topics in the Bible. But why? And how can humility transform our relationships?

My favorite definition of humility is "understanding our littleness when compared to God." We are finite. God is infinite. He knows everything. We know very little. In my relationship with God, it should be easy to admit that God is better than me. He's sinless. I sin. He loves perfectly. I don't. You get the idea. But humility isn't a quality or choice that is limited to the confines of my relationship with God. Humility should be soaked through every part of my life, including my relationships with friends and family. Jesus is the ultimate example of humility in that He was humble and obedient to the point of death. Humility means that we place the emotional, physical, and spiritual needs of others above our fleshly desire to be served, revered, and famed. We see in James 4:6-7 that God "resists the proud, but gives grace to the humble." I need more of God's grace, don't you? And I don't ever want to be in a place where God resists me. But there is something about humility that seems off-putting; we don't want to be humble. Our flesh literally rages against humility. In fact, people that are known for their humility are often the subject of jokes in worldly arenas. When you talk to little kids every day (like I do as a mother of three) the subject of fairness comes up constantly. Let's say I'm passing out treats, and one of the kids is somewhere else and hears about those treats that were distributed while they were gone. "But they got treats, I want a treat, too. It's not fair." I try to calmly explain that just because they had treats while the other child was gone doesn't mean the absentee should automatically get a treat. "You were at a birthday party with cake," I remind them. "You had cake. Your brother and sister didn't have cake. Is *that* fair?"

We might laugh at interactions like that, but we have

them with God constantly. "But God, you gave her a best friend that she gets to have all to herself, why can't I have a special relationship like that? It isn't fair." Humility doesn't demand that we be given everything someone else has been given. Pride does that. Humility reminds us that God loves us, and that should be enough. Humility is the quiet old lady at church that reminds us that we should be thankful instead of jealous. Pride is the other woman in our prayer group that loudly encourages us to be discontent and demand things from God. How thankful are we for the relationships we have? And how often do we put the needs and desires of our friends above our own the way Jesus did? I'm not just talking to you, I'm also reminding myself, because this stuff is hard. Humility is hard. I can't do it without God's help.

Ponder this: Have there been times recently when I demanded fairness from God regarding my relationships? Have I gotten upset when one friend did something for another friend that they never offered me? Is that attitude built on humility or pride? What are some ways I can help others in humility, placing their needs above my own?

Sometimes being humble means that we ask for help. I know that sounds confusing, but how often have you refused to ask someone for help because of your pride? I'm so guilty of that, and it has hurt my friends. On several occasions I have had friends tell me that they didn't feel like I valued their friendship because I never asked for their help. That made them feel like I didn't trust them. I get so obsessed with my duty to help *them* that I forget God wants us to serve *each other*. How would I feel if none of my friends ever trusted me enough to ask for my help? That sounds so lonely. It's important to realize that humility is complex, and works in more than one direction.

Ponder this: Is there someone in your life that you feel is too overwhelmed to ever help you? Can you think of the last time someone asked them for help? How would it make you feel to know that no one wanted your help?

<u>A Taste of My Own Medicine</u>
    This year has been really hard on my family. We moved to a new part of the United States to work with a church, and everything fell apart. One of the women who knew what I was going through invited me over to her house so that I would have a safe place to talk about all that had been going on. So, I shared with her. Then she completely disappeared from my life. I knew she was going through a lot, so I offered to help, but she never—not once—agreed to let *me* help *her.* It felt like a bait and switch. She had asked me to share my struggles with her and bare my soul, but she didn't trust me enough to help her with her problems or her kids. I guess I needed a taste of my own medicine before I could understand how much I had hurt my friends in the past by not letting *them* help *me.*

Prayer Time
Ask God to show you what sincere humility is. There are many examples in His Word. Pray for Him to illuminate any prideful areas in your relationships that need to change. Ask about whether God wants you to be more honest with your friends about your needs, but don't expect that they should help. As God guides you, ask and see if there is anything they can do, even if it is simply to offer their prayers and advice.

Chapter 9

LESSON NINE: ACCEPTANCE

Choose *Acceptance*...

"Be anxious for nothing, but in everything by prayer and supplication, with thanksgiving, let your requests be made known to God; and the peace of God, which surpasses all understanding, will guard your hearts and minds through Christ Jesus." -Philippians 4:6-7

"Have I not commanded you? Be strong and of good courage; do not be afraid, nor be dismayed, for the LORD your God is with you wherever you go." -Joshua 1:9

Kristin N. Spencer

I wish I could say that if you follow the biblical principles laid out in this devotional, that you will never be lonely again, but that simply isn't true. We all go through seasons where God wants to get us alone, so that we can learn more about Him, and those seasons feel lonely. It is also true that when we follow God's Word closely, we will find natural enemies in some relationships we thought were friendly. That is why acceptance is so important. When I entered my first year of college, I carried around a small slip of paper with Philippians 4:6-7 written on it and every time I felt overwhelmed, I would pull it out and read it. By the end of my first semester, the paper was worn thin and the corners were missing, but I felt that God's promise had become a daily occurrence in my life. It is important to remember that God's peace applies to our relationships as well. We are promised that God will protect our hearts and minds with Jesus when we constantly lift our anxieties to Him in prayer. This promise applies to our relationships, if we are diligent to continuously lift them to God in prayer.

One of the lessons God is trying to teach me is to come to Him first when I feel upset. I used to try to figure out which one of my friends might be a good person to confide in, but when I would tell them my heartbreaking news, I would often get a response that was less than compassionate. My friends are awesome people, so I realized that, when this happened repeatedly, God was trying to tell me something. I need to go to God first, ask Him for help, and accept that He will protect and take care of me. To be honest, this lesson has also helped my marriage, because I don't expect my husband to fix my hurt feelings for me.

Ponder this: When I feel stress or pain about what is happening in one of my relationships, where should I turn for peace?

There is also an aspect of acceptance that has to do with our lack of control. If we are honest, we will admit there isn't much we *do* control. One of the things we don't control is how other people act. When people don't want to be our friend, or they treat us poorly, it is easy to get discouraged. But God tells us that He is with us, and that we don't have to be dismayed. Accepting that we can't control the choices others make, or how they treat us, is difficult. But it is also extremely liberating. This is especially true in family relationships where there should be a natural love for one another, but that doesn't happen. Knowing that your parent doesn't love you is one of the most heartbreaking experiences possible, but once we accept there is nothing we can do to make them love us, there is freedom from the chains that once bound us to them. The truth is that God loves us, no matter what, and He loves us with a perfect love. Though we must first accept it, God's love will guide us through painful seasons, and help us to retain joy and fulfillment throughout our lives.

Ponder this: How would my attitude toward my relationships change if I approached them with the understanding that I can't control how other people act? If I accept God's perfect love, how will that shape my relationships?

<u>Things We Can't See</u>
In my family, there is a long history of different types of abuse. Many times, I have had to stop and think about the people I'm trying to love and get along with in terms of things I don't personally understand. If you had a family member with a physical injury, you would take that limitation into consideration when you thought about what they could and couldn't do, wouldn't you? I have had to learn to take emotional

injuries and past trauma into consideration when it comes to my relationships with people in my life. What do these injuries I can't see do to my family members whom I love?

Now that I'm an adult, I realize that some of my immediate family just can't love me the way God wants them to, not because they don't want to, but because they don't know how to. That's a big difference. I accept that I can't make choices for others, but I also need to accept that everyone is on an individual journey with God, and I can't expect them to behave the way I want them to, because maybe they aren't there yet. God has shown me that I need to be aware of background reasons that shape the behavior of my family members that I just can't see.

Prayer Time

Spend prayer time today asking God to show you if there are any areas in your life where you are fighting against God, refusing to accept His love or His plan. Does it make you anxious to know you aren't in control? Ask God to help you, and to show you that His promises to help you find peace are true. Pray that He will help you to realize that Him being in control is the best possible reality.

Chapter 10

LESSON TEN: JESUS

Choose *Jesus*...

"Come to Me, all you who labor and are heavy laden, and I will give you rest. Take My yoke upon you and learn from Me, for I am gentle and lowly in heart, and you will find rest for your souls. For My yoke is easy and My burden is light." - Matthew 11:28-30

"Who is he who condemns? It is Christ who died, and furthermore is also risen, who is even at the right hand of God, who also makes intercession for us." -Romans 8:34

Kristin N. Spencer

It should be the easiest decision in my life, but when I think about surrendering my burdens and hurt feelings to Jesus, my flesh wants to clutch tighter instead of release. How many of our relationships have been damaged because we demanded that another person give us rest for our souls? Only Jesus can do that. We've talked about fulfillment, expectations, and acceptance, but Jesus is the center of understanding how all of those principles fit together to create healthy relationships. As we see in Matthew 11:29, Jesus wants to teach us how to find rest in every situation we encounter in life. But this rest is conditional. It means that we have to go to Him. "Come to Me... and I will give you rest." We must go to Jesus when we need love. We should go to Jesus when we need fulfillment. When we have a hard time accepting the trials and tribulations that are part of our lives, we need to turn to Jesus. Every single day, we need to choose Jesus. There isn't anything or anyone else that will give us rest, or help us when we are weary. No one else is as gentle as Jesus. No one else can show us how to lighten our burden.

Ponder this: How many times have you resisted going to Jesus with your burdens and needs? Has this helped or hurt your relationships with others? What about your relationship with God?

Jesus does more for us than we often remember. I hope you have never been in this situation, but what if someone has unjustly accused you of something, and there is no way you can prove that those accusations aren't true? If you have experienced this and tried to explain your side of things to others, you know how pointless and discouraging it is. But we know that Jesus intercedes for us in prayer. He sees things the way they really are, and He sees into our hearts and the hearts of others. In addition to that, it says in Romans 12:15 that we shouldn't be concerned with avenging ourselves, because God knows all the circumstances and He will repay. I have experienced God being my defense when I let Him. But there is a choice involved. If we choose to avenge ourselves, then God won't. If we don't choose to take our burdens to Jesus, He won't make us. But when we make choices to leave God and Jesus out of things, we deal with the consequences.

It is also important to acknowledge that the level of intimacy we have with God and the understanding we have of His Word directly affects all of our relationships. If we don't spend time with Him daily, that influences every aspect of our lives. Each day, I need to make the same choice; I need to choose Jesus.

Ponder this: When conflict arises, how should I approach it? If God says He will be my defense, do I still have a choice in whether I let Him defend me? How does my relationship with God affect all my other relationships?

<u>Just You and Me, Jesus</u>

Earlier in the book, I mentioned that I struggle with anxiety. It has been an unwelcome commentator on my life for as far back as I can remember. Years ago, I repeatedly attempted to use my human relationships to help me deal with this anxiety. It never worked. Today, I employ a different approach: when I feel overwhelmed or anxious, I remind myself that Jesus is with me. I even say the words, "Just You and me, Jesus," out loud. Then I storm into whatever it is that has been causing my anxiety.

Whether I'm ramping up for a difficult conversation, a new and uncomfortable situation, or a brain-bending exam I know that I'm never alone. Anxiety may try to ruin my day (or my life), but the truth is that I can choose Jesus because He's already chosen me. My relationship with Him is my ultimate safe place, and your relationship with Him can be your safe place, too.

When we first moved to Pennsylvania, I had to do something I hadn't done in a really long time: try to find a traditional job. With a fancy new resumé in hand and my only suit steamed to perfection, I drove my car (what? I hadn't had my own car in over a decade) to cities I had never heard of and interviewed, over and over, in an industry I had no idea about. For some reason, most of the jobs I ended up getting called in to interview for were with insurance companies. I burst through every door with "Just You and me, Jesus," on my lips. With my background in graphic design and writing, a few companies seemed pretty sure I could learn to do the job. But as I prayed about it, I felt God telling me not to agree to any of the offers I had been getting. *What? Lord, this doesn't make any sense. I went and did this terrifying thing because my family needs me to work, what do You mean I should stay home?* But God had other plans.

Travis ended up losing his position at the church we had moved here to help, and started working full time with a painter, so that took care of our income dilemma (kind of). During that time, I also realized my kids were not dealing very well with the change of environment coupled with the loss of their beloved Papou. They needed me before and after school. Frustration filled me as I realized that God had known all along that I wouldn't be getting a traditional job, and instead would be able to work from home. Why had He made me do all of the things I absolutely hated? Drive to unknown places. Talk to strangers on the phone. Meet new people. But that was the push I needed to realize that I could be way more independent here than I was able to when we were living in Greece as missionaries. God was also preparing me for the next big adventure Travis and I would take together, right in downtown Greensburg; but that's another story for a different book.

Prayer Time

Ask God to show you how you respond to Him when He offers to give you peace. Do you go to Him, or do you try to deal with things on your own, or turn to human relationships for comfort? Pray that God would show you His faithfulness when you experience trials in your relationships. Ask Him to help you memorize important scriptures that you can hide in your heart to remember when you go through difficult seasons.

Chapter 11

PEARLS BEFORE SWINE: A WARNING

"Do not give what is holy to the dogs; nor cast your pearls before swine, lest they trample them under their feet, and turn and tear you in pieces." -Matthew 7:6

Though I hope you will be able to use the 10 biblical tools mentioned in this book for healthier relationships, I think it is also important to point out that there is an appropriate time to stop trying to improve certain relationships. There will be people who take advantage of your kindness, love, and mercy toward them. There will also be hateful people who refuse to either give or receive forgiveness. In relationships where you have repeatedly tried to use godly principles to improve things, but have failed, there is a time when it is okay to walk away. It doesn't mean that you stop loving that person, but that you no longer want them to have influence over your life because their influence isn't godly. It is not wrong to distance ourselves from people that have responded to our love and forgiveness with hatred and hostility. It is also important to remember that God does not like it when people manipulate His children, and as His children, it is right for us to end relationships that are based on another person manipulating us for their personal gain.

The wonderful principles that God has given us through His Word are precious, like pearls. God has entrusted these pearls to us, His children. And there are many people in this world who do not view these principles as precious. They don't care about these pearls. They are like the swine that Matthew 7:6 describes. This verse isn't saying that there are people that are stinky and fat like pigs, but that there is no way that a pig can appreciate pearls. When some people look at the precious principles God has given us, they don't understand why we find things like perfect love, goodness, and grace so wonderful. Because of that, there are relationships in our lives that will never improve, though we have done everything we can to better them through God's truths.

When we find ourselves in a destructive relationship that can't be improved for some reason or another, it is discouraging. But avoiding discouragement isn't a good enough reason to keep pursuing unhealthy relationships. Remember that you can always take your discouragements to God. Tell Him how you feel. He loves you, and He wants to work through your feelings with you so that He can heal you.

When Choosing Boundaries Creates Real Loss

I already mentioned that some of my familial relationships have been difficult, and several times I have had to limit my interactions with specific relatives who wouldn't respect my personal boundaries. Something that I just won't tolerate is gossip. It is so evil and destructive that I don't want it in my life. At one point, my family stateside was upset about the Syrian refugee crisis. That put me in tough situations because Travis and I were working in Athens, Greece, as missionaries at the time, and we had direct contact with many refugees that had ended up in Greece as a means of escaping their situation in Syria. I kept getting angry emails and messages that Travis and I needed to stop posting about the crisis because the United States didn't need any more immigrants.

I honestly didn't know how to respond. I still feel that as Christians, we should want to take care of others who are in need. As I physically saw thousands of displaced people without food, water, or a place to sleep, my heart was broken. I tried to explain things to those stateside the best way I could. At that time, I shared that our family was a family of immigrants to Greece. We had to apply for visas to live there. We had left our home country. The place where we lived had a main language other than English. I felt I could relate to a lot of the struggles that immigrants faced in general, and I voiced that opinion to my family members who were upset about the refugee crisis.

Several weeks later I heard one of my family members repeat a very specific phrase that I had said to one of my cousins about immigration. I asked her where she had heard that, and she told me that my cousin had mentioned it to her. I hadn't heard back from this cousin in a while, so I messaged her and asked her why she had been relating what I had said to her to other people and discussing my life when I wasn't present. Though I didn't want to argue (really), I mentioned that she was gossiping about me, and that I didn't appreciate it. I told this cousin that if she wanted to remain a part of my life, she needed to talk to *me* directly and not use my words behind my back to discuss my life with other family members. Well, she didn't like that, and we stopped talking. Several months later she died in a horrible accident.

    I had a lot of family members ask me if I regretted my decision to stop talking to her, given that she had now passed away. The truth is, I was devastated that she died (I'm still shocked and heartbroken), but I wasn't sad about maintaining my boundary. I even thought that maybe I would *get* upset about cutting off communication with her as time passed and we all grieved her death, but I didn't. I had always been open to reconciliation, but she hadn't been, and that was outside of my control. If I had to do it all over again, I would still make the same choices I did back then.

CHAPTER 12

HOLY SEX REBOOT - PREVIEW

Written by T. E. Spencer and Kristin N. Spencer

Chapter 1: Double the Brokenness

A huge part of our testimony as a couple is that both of us had sex outside of marriage before meeting and then had sex with each other before marriage once we did get together. If I could shake young people and tell them one thing, it would be to abstain from sexual immorality because its effects are damaging and long-lasting. It seems to me that there is an idea floating through the body of believers that once you get married, all the natural consequences of past sexual sin will dissipate into thin air. That couldn't be further from the truth. Past sexual sin chases you into your marriage, and after the honeymoon period is over, it threatens to tear your marriage apart from the inside out.

POV - Kristin
Sitting in the middle of my bed, positioned against the wall beneath a large window with happy sunlight streaming in, my sixteen-year-old self debated the ethics of the choice before her. She chose to push them into the trash bin of in her mind as thoughts to be later discarded. Ethics didn't matter anymore, she thought. God seemed far away and apathetic. Seated atop the fluffy gray bedspread with white floral outlines, she wrote her decision in a yellow journal covered in smiley faces. A matching black and white pen, also adorned with floral smileys recorded these words, "I just want to feel loved. That can't be so bad, can it?"

When I was sixteen years old, I gave my virginity to my high school sweetheart. He wasn't a Christian, so he had no objections. I was looking for male love and affection. My family environment had been marred by an admission of my father that he'd been having serial affairs over the previous ten years. On my sixteenth birthday, my dad temporarily moved out of our house. To be honest, although the idea of sex was exciting because of the taboo associated with it, I never really felt much physical pleasure when I had sex with my boyfriend. Later I realized my main benefit from our sexual relationship was that he would cuddle me and tell me he loved me after we had had sex. That was something I craved. The low point was my dad's catching us having sex after he moved back in. It was so cliché that I wanted to laugh, but that hardly seemed appropriate. I sat in the living room on a sea foam green couch alone while both parents sat on the adjacent, matching couch, sitting together but not touching. They lectured me about "not having sex," and I remember thinking that my dad was such a hypocrite. Defying him seemed to be an added benefit of my sexual misbehavior.

After my boyfriend broke up with me, I decided not to have sex again until I was married. I spent my time focusing on finishing high school, getting my university degree, and growing closer to Jesus. When I wasn't at practice for my collegiate rowing team, I was at school, work, or church, where I spent several hours each week volunteering in the Junior High Center. Three semesters before graduation, I met Travis through a new Internet phenomenon all the colleges were using, Facebook. His profile popped up when I clicked on the hyperlinked title of my favorite band, The O. C. Supertones. He was working on staff at a church near his home in Westminster while finishing his degree in Criminal Justice at the same university I attended. There were so many things that I found attractive about him, but the main one was his love for Jesus. The second most wonderful thing about him was the way he made me laugh. I remember rubbing my face after our dates because my cheeks were sore from smiling. He was a hard worker, kind, involved in ministry, and he liked me. I couldn't believe he liked me, especially when there was a line of girls who wanted to date him. He was pretty naïve and didn't realize all of the dirty looks and rude comments I endured from his other admirers. For a while, we were super paranoid about purity. Travis sat me down one night to confess to me that he was not a virgin. We were at my house in the living room, and I clutched a pillow to my chest for comfort. He confessed that he had been engaged to a woman before he met me, and they had been sexually active throughout their relationship. I think he expected me to get upset that he had already had sex, but instead I stunned him with my own confession. Both of us cried and talked late into the night before Travis left to go home. We both agreed that we wanted to move forward with our relationship despite the failures from our individual pasts.

 We were watching some weird film I had to write about for my feminism class one night, and after that he held my hand, and we gave each other Eskimo kisses (some serious nose on nose action) for about an hour. Yes, super cheesy, I know. Then he asked if it was ok if he kissed me. It was so romantic. Of course I said yes! Once we started kissing, everything went downhill. Before that, we had depended on rules and legalism to protect us from our lustful hearts instead of dealing with the lust issues neither of us had ever overcome. For a while we still abstained from sex, but as our wedding date grew closer, we gave into our temptations and had sex several times. One time in particular I remember Travis went to buy condoms down the street from my parents' house. He turned his shirt inside out because it had a Bible verse on it. Suffice it to say that was definitely a low point. After our confession to the pastor who was going to officiate our wedding ceremony, he told us that he wanted us to take a two-week break from any kind of communication. The two weeks apart were good but difficult. We still never really worked through the heart issues that had led to our sexual sin. Travis was still dealing with his struggle against pornography addiction (which he had told me about), and I was still struggling with intense feelings of worthlessness. Two months before our wedding, we agreed not to touch at all, hoping that God could restore all the brokenness our sexual sin had caused in our walks with Him and also in our relationship with each other.

The day after our wedding at a resort where we spent our two-day honeymoon, we were sitting on a purple chaise lounge watching *Must Love Dogs*. Travis swatted my hand away when I attempted to touch him. When I realized it was out of habit, I cried for two hours. It was apparent in that moment that all the damage of our pre-marital sex had followed us into our marriage. There were also trust issues between us. I didn't trust Travis to make important decisions for us as a couple because I knew that he could be easily swayed into sin the way he had been when he had sex with me before we got married. Add that to Travis's pornography and lust problems, which he started to indulge again a few months into our marriage, and you can imagine how miserable our first years together were. [End of POV]

POV - Travis
I was nine years old crouching in a circle in an abandoned driveway of our neighborhood when I had my first encounter with pornography. My friend took a porno magazine from his father's closet, and we sat there ogling those naked women on the glossy pages. Feelings, awakened by peer pressure, shaped my views on sexuality long before any Christian adult figure could guide me into God's truths. From that point on it was a downhill slide. A constant struggle against learning what we must not do while continuing to fight the fleshly desires within. As I grew older, I was more secretive and savvy about how I could fulfill my lustful cravings with pornography and masturbation. All the while, I was caught in the endless cycle of: sin, shame, and repentance. This continued into adulthood. There were periods of victory with the cause being not always so spiritual.

When I was fifteen years old, I transferred from a public school into a private Christian school. It was there that I met a girl who was a class below me. We became friends, and when she graduated, we dated. The relationship progressed rapidly in nature with no sexual limits. That whole time I was persistent in my pornography habit. I saved up enough money to buy a ring so I could propose to her. After she said yes, we celebrated with sex later that night. Through that relationship, which lasted around one and a half years, I was in that same cycle of sin, shame, and repentance. I would try, in my strength, to make the relationship go in a God honoring direction, but I always failed. At the end, once and for all, God convicted me to end the relationship and turn to Him. I was absolutely exhausted from living a lie: going to church and serving while living my transgressing life in secret. I broke off the engagement and ended the relationship. How I selfishly led that relationship with my desires will forever be a reminder of how my actions can devastate others. Even now I am realizing that what I did in that relationship was manipulative and abusive. For all intents and purposes, I was an abuser.

During the next year I devoted my life to God. I ceased indulging in all pornography and masturbation and focused on others instead of myself. I tried to educate myself with God's Word, paying attention to how it applies to my life and others' lives. At the end of that year, my future wife messaged me through Facebook. It was college in 2005 when DSL was a luxury and Facebook was for colleges only. Don't judge, ok? We messaged back and forth for several months before agreeing to meet in person at the homeless ministry where I served. It was like, so *Sleepless in Seattle*, just with the Empire State Building being a gazebo in Garden Grove and the elevator attendant being her friend Sar and without my being a widower with a child. OK, so it isn't really like that movie. I just want to be Tom Hanks.

You Can Do Better

After we met, our relationship moved toward marriage quite quickly. The cloud of my past cast a dark shadows over our relationship. I did my best to lead the relationship in a godly way, but my lust soon returned. The year of abstaining from everything didn't do the trick. We had a sexual relationship, and it felt like my earlier one all over again. After a while, Kristin and I confessed it to our pastor, and he prescribed a two-week break from all communications. I read *No Compromise*, the Keith Green story, and tried to right the wrongs in my relationship with God. The time that passed between meeting Kristin and marrying her was only ten months.

Since my sexual desires were awakened at nine years old, and the Church had only talked about sex or sexuality as if it were "he who must not be named," I didn't really know how to deal with sex as a Christian other than "to not to." So, as most Christians, I viewed marriage as the legal and therefore godly way of being able to have sex. But this view was dangerous. After our honeymoon, my unresolved issues with pornography and my family history of divorce skewed my chance to give the beginning of our marriage the start it deserved. [End of POV]

At this point, we have been married for over eleven years. Five years ago we made the decision to address the different problems in our marriage and emphasized communication and honesty about sexual sin. We embarked on our own holy sex reboot, and the way it has improved our relationship is amazing. We have never been closer to God or each other, despite the constant trials we have faced. Kristin and I wondered what it would be like if we were completely honest with each other about everything. We each faced our individual struggles but with mutual support. I needed to relearn everything the Bible taught about the purpose and boundaries of sex while Kristin wrestled with believing God's love was enough to override her feelings of worthlessness. We also set up more realistic boundaries in our relationship that would better protect us from outside influences, and we each confessed temptations when they first happened.

During this process, we recognized that we needed to deal with the emotional baggage left over from our childhoods, as that had shaped the way we viewed each other. I was paralyzed by the fear that Kristin would leave me while she was paranoid that I would cheat. We realized that these fears were rooted in witnessing similar events in our parents' lives.

Using the Bible and countless long, uncomfortable but fruitful conversations, God helped us transform our marriage into something we could have never imagined. The main benefit of this process is a tangibly changed individual walk with the Lord. We hope that the same process that worked for each of us will help you find healing.

Write it down.

Make a journal entry titled, "My Sexual Testimony" and write your own testimony of your ideas about sex and any sexual immorality in which you have taken part. It will help you later on when you try to understand how your past has influenced the way you view sex.

Acknowledgements

There is always a group of people working behind the scenes for any project to comes to fruition.

I want to thank my husband, Travis, for his unwavering support and for helping me learn a lot of these lessons.

Thank you to my children, I love you guys so much. I hope one day you can use all of the things God is teaching Mommy so that you can have your own healthy relationships.

A big thanks to my editor, Maria Mountokalaki. Her pen is a sword.

Thank you, Lise Cartwright, my amazing coach.

To my launch team, you all rock.

Also, to my extended family (including my supportive friends), love you.

About the Author

Kristin N. Spencer spends part of each day imagining up new worlds and beings when she isn't busy taking care of her three children and writing partner husband T. E. Spencer. When she's not writing you can find her working in full time ministry, sewing cosplay costumes, or watching geekesque movies. She writes whatever genre she wants including but not limited to Non-Fiction, Contemporary Fiction, Sci-Fi, Space Fantasy, and traditional Fantasy. Kristin studied Comparative World Literature at California State University, Long Beach and received a Bachelors, which she fondly calls a degree in reading. Her favorite movie is Sabrina (the Julia Ormond version) and her favorite person is Jesus.

She has worked in full time ministry for the last eight years, and also runs the women's discipleship website *Sincerely Adorned*.

OTHER BOOKS BY AUTHOR

Christian Nonfiction
You Aren't Worthless: Unlock the Truth to Godly Confidence
Holy Sex Reboot: My Sexual Identity in Christ (coauthored by T. E. Spencer)
Updated edition coming 11/10/2019
Confident Nobody (Subtitle TBA)
Coming 1/12/2020

Fiction
<u>The Desires and Decisions Series</u>
(Middle Grade to YA)
Newfangled
Flummoxed
Kerfuffle

<u>The Plunge Into Darkness Series</u>
(Recommended age: 16+)
Plunge Into Darkness
The Knotted Woman (*Coming April 2020*)
The Chorus of the Fallen (*Coming May 2020*)

Your Free Relationship Diagnostic Tool
Because I want to help you implement the relationship tools in this book, I have created a five-minute flowchart that will help you determine whether the relationships in your life are in need of some work, are God-centered, or are unhealthy. To sign up to get your free printable Relationship Diagnosis Tool, go to youcandobetterbook.com/free

In addition to your free flowchart, you will also get fun email updates and more free stuff. I hope you check it out.

www.ingramcontent.com/pod-product-compliance
Lightning Source LLC
Chambersburg PA
CBHW052119110526
44592CB00013B/1670